EVERYONE

— IS A —

CEO

CUSTOMER EXPERIENCE ORIGINATOR

KEVIN THOMPSON MPA DTM

First Edition

Printed in 2015 in the United States of America

Book designed by Ian Berg

ISBN 13: 978-0-996-26270-5

DEDICATION

This book is dedicated to DJ and Jeremiah.

Delight yourself in the Lord, and he will give
you the desires of your heart.

Psalm 37:4

Table of Contents

INTRODUCTION

HAVE YOU EVER had a horrible customer service experience? How many people did you tell about it? Did you decide that was the last time you would spend your hard-earned money at that place of business?

If your answer is yes, then you understand the value of ensuring that this doesn't happen to your organization.

Are you interested in learning how to not only prevent horrible customer service experiences but also provide experiences that are so unique that they separate your organization from your closest competitor? Everyone Is a CEO is a customer experience process that empowers organizations to tap into their innovation and creativity and improve their bottom lines. This book will challenge you, your staff, and your organization to be your best and authentic selves. Opportunities to improve brand awareness and market share await you.

Turn the page and learn how your organization will benefit from the strategies and insights provided in Everyone Is a CEO.

CHAPTER 1

Most Businesses Suffer from a Lack of Good Customer Service

IT WAS MY THIRD time in less than three weeks entering 3 Guys Auto Service Store. I went there initially because my car's battery light came on. The 3 Guys staff members connected my car's computer to their diagnostic computer to analyze the problem. They informed me that there was nothing wrong with the battery or charging system and then reset the computer. There was no charge. Great service, I thought. Wouldn't you think the same? A week later, the battery light came on again, and the car stopped running while I was driving on the highway. I called a roadside assistance company, and an hour and a half later, I returned to 3 Guys Auto Service Store. In an effort to prevent the staff members from assuring me that the car was fine, I asked that they replace the battery. An hour later, they told me the car was fine. I asked whether they replaced the battery. They said no. I asked them again to replace the battery. (Warning sign: they did not listen to me the first time I asked them to replace the battery.) They took the car back into the garage, and forty-five minutes later, the battery was replaced.

Three days later, the car stopped running, and the battery light came on again. I took the car to the manufacturer's service department, and the technicians told me the battery that 3 Guys installed had a bad cell. In addition, they recommended changing the alternator. They fixed the problem and recommended that I return the battery to 3 Guys for a refund. I returned to 3 Guys carrying a heavy car battery in my arms. Three people were ahead of me in line for the service desk. Twenty minutes later, I finally reached the service staff member. After I explained my ordeal, the service staff member directed me to the parts section at the rear of the store. I carried the heavy battery to the rear of the store only to have the salesperson in parts direct me back to the service staff. Refusing to be bounced back and forth, I asked to speak with the store manager. The parts salesperson, in a rude tone of voice, called the manager. After explaining the problem, the manager directed me to the cashier to obtain a refund. Although I achieved my goal of getting a refund, the process left me with a bad feeling, and I am not sure I will ever take my car there for service again. I would not be surprised if the "3 Guys" of the 3 Guys Auto Service Store turned out to be Moe, Larry, and Curly from the Three Stooges. This is what poor customer service looks and feels like to your customers.

Most organizations suffer from a lack of good customer service. This is mainly because they are not aware of any problems with their customer service. If one of these organizations is your competitor, this is a golden opportunity for you to use your knowledge from reading this book to gain the upper hand. I am going to help you navigate the world of establishing a customer experience work culture. We will discuss a few misconceptions about customer service as well as tools and strategies you can use to beat the competition.

What is customer service?

Many people describe customer service as a transaction between the staff of an organization and its customers. The misconception is that some organizations believe transactional service is good customer service.

When you go to the ATM, do you think of it as good customer service or a transaction? You walk up to the machine and insert your card, enter your pass code, and either deposit or withdraw money. There is no customer service associated with the visit to the ATM. It is a just a transaction. A service requires some kind of interpersonal interaction.

Personal interaction is the heart of good customer service. The quality of customer service is a perception created in the minds of the customer and the staff. It is easy for your staff members to believe they have delivered good customer service and for your customers to consider the same service to be less than adequate. How do you bridge the gap of perception between your staff and your customers? Even more important, how do you take advantage of the fact that your competition may not even be aware of its own customer service gap?

The process of transforming customer service from a mere transaction into an experience can be found in the details. For us to achieve this transformation from a service into an experience, we need to look at the journey your organization has taken.

Let's begin by answering the following questions:

What does your organization do differently today compared with when you started working there?

What things changed?

When and why did they change?

What was the market like in your industry when you started working at your organization, and how did it change over time?

How many changes has your organization made over the years to stay current with advancements in the market?

These are important questions for reflection when you are thinking about establishing a work culture centered on customer experience and the value that your organization brings to the market.

I recommend that you make a list of answers to the above questions. Take time to reflect before answering these questions. Consider not only where your organization has been but also which direction you need to go in the near future to stay ahead of changes in the market.

This leads us to the next question.

What are you doing as it relates to customer service, and how are you measuring it?

Not taking the time to look at what your organization is doing and how you measure it is like trying to drive a car with your eyes closed. With any luck, you may get to your destination as long as you are not going too far. But if there is a turn in the road, the car is not aligned correctly, the steering wheel is not straight when you start, another car is on the road ahead of you, or a person jumps in front of your car, you will have an accident. The metaphor of driving with your eyes closed is intended to reveal a hidden truth. While we may think of an accident as an unforeseen circumstance, the truth is that there is a high probability we are going to be in an accident because our eyes are closed. We would have seen these obstacles if we had our eyes open and we were watching for them. Similarly, the benefits of a customer experience versus a customer service transaction work culture can be identified if you are looking for them.

What does your customer service look like, and how do you measure it?

Think of the indicators you would use to measure the outcomes that your customers experience when they come to your organization. Think of the things they see. By walking in the footsteps of your customers, you will start to see things that you might overlook as an executive manager.

How do your staff members feel about the service they provide?

Are staff members excited about the jobs they are doing, or do they see them as routine?

How you answer these questions has a tremendous effect on how customers experience service in your organization.

You should also consider the communication culture within your organization. How do people communicate? Do they make eye contact? Do they greet one another at the start of the day? If your answer is no, these people may be treating your customers in the same manner, which is a serious issue. Staff members are less likely to treat customers better than they treat other staff members. An observation of the exchange of simple pleasantries between staff members can be a window view into your organization's customer experience.

Would you say your organization has open communication, where information is openly shared between and within departments?

If you answer no or that you do not know whether this is a major problem, or if you believe your organization has a culture that promotes open communication, how do you know? This brings us back to the previous question. What do you think your customers experience and how do you measure it? We will have a deeper discussion providing specific strategies to help answer these questions later in the book.

Do your staff members feel comfortable discussing possible alternatives to the way they are currently working with their manager?

This is an interesting question. If an alternate view about how business is conducted is welcomed in your organization, how do you track and monitor it? Who decides if people take action? Is there a formal process for this information to be distributed throughout the organization, or is it practice to give a nod and a smile without taking any action? Do supervisors, managers, and line staff members meet on a regular basis to discuss trends in the market and what they see in their daily work, or is the culture within your organization made up of multiple silos? Even if one department depends on another in the logical progression of product and/or services development, do they talk with each other? If management, supervisors, and staff are not talking to one another in an open forum, you might be able to provide a better customer experience just by making that change. This may be an opportunity for you to improve the quality of customer service in your organization and increase productivity at the same time.

The bottom-line question is: What is the communication culture of your organization?

Even more important, how do you change this communication culture to improve customer experiences?

The best answers to these questions and how to leverage them into a strategy to improve your customers' experiences are the types of insights that you will learn going forward.

Most organizations suffer from a lack of good customer service, and that is the bad news. The good news is, it may require small changes in your processes to enhance the experience perceptions of your customers. First impressions are the most lasting. By making a small change in the customer's first encounter with your organization, you can begin to frame the experience the customer will have.

A genuine smile from your staff can make all the difference in how your organization is perceived when the customer first walks through the door. Why do I say genuine? Too many times, I have seen staff members in different organizations say, "So glad that you are here at XYZ organization. May I help you?" But the look in their eyes reveals that their words are empty. It is just a script or line that someone devised. The staff may not have had any input into the development of the initial customer conversation. If the customer feels that the staff member is not genuine, the customer will be able to tell right away. Trust and the potential sale of products are lost, in addition to damaging the reputation of the organization.

The goal is to develop a work culture that embraces open communication among all levels of staff. In addition, you want to empower your staff to accept responsibility for creating a positive customer experience. This will not only enhance the experience your customers receive, but it also will foster an environment where innovation and new offerings can develop. Developing this type of work culture provides a marked advantage over your competition. The fact is that most of your competitors are not looking to develop a customer experience. Deciding to develop your customer experience work culture places your organization ahead of the curve and positioned to be a thought leader in your industry.

The most exciting thing of all is that your customers benefit immediately from this type of communication and culture change. Your customers feel that your organization cares about them and considers them special because of the attention they receive from your staff. This attention to detail at every level of the organization develops into a transformational customer experience and gives you an advantage over your competition.

Investing the time and resources into creating this type of work culture can completely eliminate the competition. You can accomplish this by having your staff develop a customer experience mind-set. If your staff members thought of themselves as owners of your organization, what decisions would they make? What would they do differently to ensure they retained current customers and attracted new ones? This is the beginning of your staff thinking like a CEO, an organization owner.

The organization-owner mind-set is focused on customer experience. Your staff members need to become different CEOs. They need to think of themselves as Customer Experience Originators. The customer experience begins with interactions with your staff, and it sets the tone for how the customer perceives your organization. If your staff members' mind-sets are focused on providing the best customer experience possible, then they have the opportunity to continue to improve on the product (experience) they provide. If there is a culture of open communication throughout the organization where all staff members are focused on providing the best outcome for the customer, then opportunities to provide an exceptional customer experience increase exponentially.

Why should your staff be focused on customer experience rather than customer service?

People connect more with the experience they have than with the service they receive. This is why at the end of every Super Bowl when someone asks the Most Valuable Player of the game what he is going to do after winning the Super Bowl, the player replies, "I'm going to Disney World!" Besides the fact that Disney paid for the commercial time, why would the MVP or anyone else want to go to Disney? Let me tell you why. I have visited Disney World more than ten times in ten consecutive years. It is the customer experience that has me return so often. Some people think of it as customer service, but that is only scratching the surface.

The first thing I noticed about Disney World was the cleanliness. As I walked around, I noticed no litter on the grounds. Do you know why? It is every employee's job to keep the grounds clean. Sure, Disney has staff assigned to keep the grounds clean, but regardless of role, any staff member who sees litter picks it up. Imagine if your staff had that type of dedication to the customer experience at your organization. Remember, we spoke about your staff making the first impression. The Disney staff started to frame my view as a customer by ensuring nothing was out of place and everything looked clean.

The second thing I noticed were the uniforms of the Disney staff. The uniforms were consistent with the theme of the area where each worked. Disney made sure that I never saw an astronaut or fairy-tale character in Frontierland. There was a high sense of congruency with the staff members' uniforms and the characters, which established a level of trust. It was subtle, but it was there.

The third thing I noticed were the smells. I believe the Disney team controlled certain aromas in specific areas to evoke specific feelings and emotions. Now I am not suggesting that you need to follow suit in your organization, but I want to highlight the attention to detail that Disney has gone to create a specific type of experience for its customers. I think this is the real magic of Disney. This is why people want to go there. This is why just the mention of the name makes people young and old smile. Would you like your customers to think of your organization in the same way? It is possible, but it takes commitment, open communication, a customer experience mind-set, an organizational culture that will support and reward this behavior, as well as dedication of time and resources to ensure success.

One of the things you may want to consider is how your organization is going to measure customer experience. To start, you will need to assess where your organization is and what actions you are taking in regard to customer service. This step may be sobering. You may discover some things you wish you had not, but I promise you the time and energy you put into it will be well worth the effort. You can accomplish this in several ways.

Consider hiring a secret shopper to visit your organization. A secret shopper is an outside consultant who plays the role of a customer and documents the experience. This is a great way to discover what works well and what needs improvement. I have had the pleasure of being a secret shopper for several organizations, and the results were eye opening. One of them was an organization that provided food and shelter for those who were homeless. The staff members with whom I came into contact had all seen me before dressed in a suit and tie when

I met with the CEO. To be congruent with the customer role I would play as a secret shopper, I did not shave for several days, I put on a pair of old sneakers and dirty jeans, and I did not brush my teeth that morning. I took off all my jewelry, including my watch, and anything else that looked expensive. I noticed that my rings had left noticeable indentations in my fingers, so I was prepared to tell a story to the intake worker about how I was beaten and my rings were stolen from me. I went outside and put dirt on my hands and under my nails. Did I mention I did not shower?

Everything about me said homeless man. I walked into the organization with my head down and was careful not to make eye contact. I took a posture and mind-set of someone who felt defeated. I was soft-spoken and appeared to be ashamed that I was there.

When the intake worker took me into her cubicle, I refused to make eye contact with her. She asked how she could help me, and I walked her through a series of incidents that led me to this apparent point in my life. She was kind and compassionate. She offered me food and told me that the person with whom I would have to speak about obtaining shelter was a manager who was in a meeting.

I waited for close to two hours for the manager to come out to speak with me. When the manager saw me, she looked disgusted. She was mean and nonprofessional. She treated me as less than a person and told me I would have to wait another hour before she could help me. This was a sunny September day, so waiting outside was not a problem for me.

After hearing the manager, the intake worker came back to apologize and asked if I wanted some juice or water. I thanked her for being so kind and told her I would return. I left, documented the incident, and went to see the CEO the following day. My role was so convincing that no one, not even the intake worker, recognized me as the homeless person when I arrived. The CEO of the organization was shocked by my experience the previous day. He had set me up to be registered with the intake worker who he thought was the organization's biggest problem. Not only was he surprised that she was so attentive and caring to me but doubly surprised that the manager treated me in such a poor manner.

When I shared the secret-shopping customer experience during the training, the intake worker who took care of me shared that she was so upset about my homelessness that she shared my experience with her husband. Everyone cheered, because the intake worker provided the customer experience they all aspired to share. The manager who treated me so poorly as a homeless man was shocked at my transformation and the story I shared. She was the supervisor of the intake worker that management believed provided poor customer experience. The real secret of the secret shopper identified the manager of the intake worker as providing a poor customer experience. Although the manager attended the training, I did not mention our interaction with me as a homeless man during the training. This manager ended up being employed elsewhere. This is the value of engaging a consultant to be a secret shopper in your organization.

The television show Undercover Boss uses another way of personally finding out what does and does not work to ensure a great customer experience. This concept is the same as the secret shopper, but instead of hiring someone else, you become the secret shopper. This may require a little coaching and instruction, but you can see a number of things about your organization through the eyes of the customer.

Another way to assess the customer experience in your organization is through surveys. You can use post-purchase surveys that are sent via e-mail. You can use telephone surveys or customer point-of-contact surveys. One of the biggest issues with surveys is that they may seem intrusive to the customer and turn a relatively good experience sour. To avoid this, be careful how questions are worded and do not ask too many questions. Make the survey quick and easy to answer, give the customer the opportunity to opt in, and if you want a high response rate, offer something of value for taking the survey and let the customer know up front what the valuable offer is.

All these strategies will help provide answers that concern you most about the customer experience in your organization. Assessing the customer experience also can give you an upper hand on your competitors who are not doing it and may not be aware of their own issues. One of the best ways for you to find out how weak or strong your competitors are in comparison with your organization is to secret-shop them. The information you gather can be invaluable as you determine your next strategic moves. What do you see that can give your competitors advantages over your organization? This is an important aspect of a SWOT (strength, weakness, opportunity, threat) analysis. I highly recommend that you make a SWOT analysis part of your strategic goal setting. It gives you the opportunity to objectively look at where your organization is positioned in the marketplace and what is the best direction for you to go.

What have you heard your customers say about your competition? If you are not sure, ask them. "Why did you come to see us today, and how can we make your experience better?" "What could we offer that would be beneficial, saving you time and money?" "How can we be your organization of choice compared with XYZ Company?" These are a few of the types of inquiries you can make to help gain insight into the experiences your customers have with you.

What type of press has your competition received? The adage "any press is good press" is just not true. Bad press can give you insight into where you might be able to edge out your competition in market share, especially if it is an area in the industry where you are doing well. Bad press can reveal a segment that is underserved by the competition. Put the competitor's name in your favorite Internet search engine with the words "poor or bad customer service" and see what comes up. Another place to check is the Better Business Bureau, or the local or state chamber of commerce. These resources can provide a real inside view into the inner workings of the customer service culture of your competition.

EVERYONE IS A CEO

CHAPTER 2

Customers Think Service but Want the Experience

THERE IS A DIFFERENCE between service and experience. People commonly think of customer service not as an experience, but it is the experience that keeps them coming back or sends them to the competition. The customer usually gets the service but may never have an experience. Every staff member has an opportunity to make a real impact on transforming transactional service into an encounter that becomes an experience that the customer raves about to friends.

The question is, do the staff members understand the importance of their roles?

Many times, the answer to this question is no. I worked with a team of fifty customer service staff members who had the worst customer service and employee-satisfaction scores in an organization. My training and development tools transformed this organization to rank it at the top in surveys for customer service and employee satisfaction. One of the keys to this transformation was instilling in staff members' minds the value of the roles they played in the success of the organization. All of them came to see themselves as Customer Experience Originators (CEOs) and transformed transactional services into experiences that customers raved about. They understood how first impressions affected the customer and set the tone for the entire experience. They learned what aspects of their customer service would become transactional and made conscious choices to turn them into experiences.

Did things go wrong in the customers' journey from transaction to experience? Sure they did, but what made the difference was the way the staff reacted to each problem. In a customer service mind-set, the staff would have considered the issue someone else's problem. In the Customer Experience Originator mind-set, staff members showed genuine care and concern for the customer even if their department was not directly involved. They became advocates and partners with the customers to ensure they had the best experience possible even if something went wrong.

The customers noticed the difference and started to tell others about it. The idea of having a Customer Experience Originator mind-set began to grow and be embraced by staff outside of this department. People enjoyed what they were doing and looked forward to coming to work. The entire culture of the department changed and started to change others. That is the value of staff understanding the difference between transactional customer service and transformational customer experience and the roles they play in the process.

The change of mind-set resulted in shared happiness among all involved. Coworkers who once hardly spoke to each other would brainstorm to determine how they could have a better impact on the customers' experiences. Everyone noticed that they naturally smiled more, which made the customers smile more. I am not talking about a fake smile. I am speaking of a genuine smile. One of the major changes identified in the transformation of the department's culture was that staff members started to care about one another. They thought of ways to make other people's days easier. Workers who needed help did not have to ask for it. Fellow staff members started to anticipate one another's needs. This resulted in an office that ran more smoothly and productively. If a staff member called in sick, everyone else would pitch in to ensure that person's work was completed. Management did not have to ask. Staff took responsibility and made things happen. The CEO mind-set change made everyone smile. Every staff member knew that their coworkers had their backs and vice versa. They became one big happy family, and the customers noticed this culture as soon as they entered the organization. Happiness became contagious. If this is the first impression your customers have when they enter your organization, they feel at ease and look forward to their visit. When your staff is focused on providing an experience and not merely a transactional service, everyone can sense it.

Providing transactional service to your customers is ordinary. Turning that service into an experience makes your organization extraordinary and can position it to be a leader in the industry. Your organization becomes known as a place where people receive a high level of value from your staff members because of the CEO mind-set. Your staff will engage your customers and pay close attention to their needs, wants, and desires. When your staff members pay close attention to the needs of your customers, your sales increase and so does customer satisfaction.

If you guessed the converse is true, you are correct. The customer may not perceive the true value of what you do if your staff provides mere transactional customer service without the experience. It is the experience that enhances the value of what you have to offer in the customers' minds.

It is like the experience of buying a car. Have you ever considered buying a car without test-driving it? Why not? The car is a utility of transportation and will take you from one destination to another. If this is all the customer wants, there would be no need for a test-drive. But in the customer's mind, it is all about the journey.

Let's be honest about buying a car. If you are like me, you are first interested in what the car looks like. What is the shape? How many doors does it have? Is it a hatchback, SUV, or sedan? What is your major reasons to use it? Will you be driving an hour or more a day to your job or will you be spending most of the day in the vehicle as part of your job? What color do you like? What color do you not like? Do you want cloth or leather seats? Are the seats heated? Air conditioning, AM/FM stereo radio, CD player, MP3 player, Bluetooth connection, ABS brakes? I could go on, but you get the idea.

So what do these things have to do with arriving at my destination? Nothing really impactful. I can arrive at my destination without a number of items that the car dealer calls options, but the experience has everything to do with how I feel during my journey to the destination. It is this feeling, or my perception of the experience, that I am sold when buying a car. The various options give me the experience I desire every time I drive the car. Do you understand it now? Developing your staff members to embrace a CEO (Customer Experience Originator) mind-set will provide them with a number of options that they think the customer may like and in doing so increase the value of the experience in your organization.

It is like Disney World. Customers do not look at Disney as a service organization, which it truly is, but Disney has become known for consistently providing great experiences, and that is why people go there. How proud would you feel if people came to think of your organization in the same light? That is what turning a mere transactional service into an experience is all about.

"Customer service" is a commonly used term. Transforming the service into an experience makes the journey uniquely suited for each customer. It is attention to detail and intimate knowledge of your customer that provides an opportunity for customization that transforms a service into an experience. If you provide customer service, the best you can become is good. Changing the service mind-set into a Customer Experience Originator (CEO) mind-set provides an opportunity to have customers perceive you as exceptional.

A number of organizations have become complacent and set their goals to being as good if not a little better than their competitors. If you take this type of approach, it will not give your organization the opportunity to become an industry leader. Your organization will feel like it is in a constant state of trying to catch up. How can your organization be an industry leader if you are following a path that someone else has made? Sure, the trip may not be as bumpy, but you will not arrive at your desired destination faster than the person in front of you. You need to be a trailblazer. Now, I am not saying that you should not take advantage of the opportunity to learn from your competition. By all means, learn what is and is not working, but you need to make an assessment of where you are as well and how you can take advantage of what you find to blaze a different trail that will attract customers.

Making a decision to be the same as your competition shows a lack of creativity and innovation. Will you make mistakes along the way? Sure you will. Thomas Edison failed thousands of times before he found out how to make a lightbulb work. Although you may not have to try as hard as he did to get it right, you must share the same level of determination and dedication to reaching your destination. The best part is that once you begin to see the light (pun intended) about providing customer experiences, you will notice that your organization becomes more flexible, your staff members tap into their collective knowledge, their creative juices begin to follow, communication improves at every level among departments, and excitement fills the air. You will see people who once provided transactional service doing exceptional things to assist customers and coworkers. As a result, you will notice your organization move forward in ways you could not have imaged. That is the excitement of adopting the CEO mind-set.

The CEO mind-set also provides the opportunity for your organization to separate itself from the competition, because it is perceived as unique. What makes Disney World different from other theme parks? A consistent message and theme. Regardless of the Disney park you visit, you will notice that everyone and everything is aligned with the theme for that area. Let's take a look at Disney World's first theme park, Magic Kingdom.

The first thing is the name. "Magic Kingdom" suggests that you are going to experience something magical and see royalty. The reality is the magic that you do not see, and the royalty is you. Disney has gone to every length to roll out the red carpet for you. The magic that is hidden is an entire city underneath the Magic Kingdom that allows for movement of food products, merchandise, staff members, and Disney characters. The magic is that you never see any food delivery from the street to the restaurants, trucks collecting garbage, or characters out of place. Even though Frontierland is right next to Snow White's castle, you will never see Snow White in Frontierland. That is not where she belongs. She belongs near, in, and around the castle. So how does Snow White get from the dressing room to the castle without going through Frontierland? She uses the underground passageways that connect all the sections of the Magic Kingdom. By ensuring that the right characters are seen only in the right sections of the park, Disney provides its customers with a feeling of consistency and congruence.

It is this type of attention to detail—understanding your customers' needs and consistency in your message—that is key to providing a unique experience that will separate your organization from your competition.

Why is this type of separation from others in the industry so important?

This is where your organization becomes known for something that your competition is not. This is where your organization transcends what it does (service) and becomes known for what it provides (the experience). Customer experience is one area in which your competitors can never defeat you, because you and your organization are unique. Your organization must focus on how to give each customer the best experience possible. When you and your staff make customer experience the focus for your organization, you will notice that—like Disney—your organization will become known for what you provide, not what you do.

Once your organization embraces the Customer Experience Originator (CEO) culture, it will feel like magic, and you will be treating your customers like royalty. Your staff and customers will both have that perception. Innovation and creativity will become commonplace among staff. Your organization will establish a new normal: a Customer Experience Originator (CEO) normal. When knowing what to do becomes second nature to your employees, your organization has developed a truly engaged staff that embraces the Customer Experience Originator (CEO) work culture.

Most customers feel this type of experience is rare. Think about it. How often during your visits to other organizations do you feel that the staff members are displaying magical moments and treating customers like royalty?

Your brand identity can either benefit from good customer experience or suffer without it. Having your organization recognized as one that provides a Customer Experience Originator (CEO) culture will create a buzz not only with your customers and their friends but with your competitors as well. If you do not make a decision to pursue a Customer Experience Originator (CEO) work culture, you risk losing the opportunity to transform your organization into something exceptional. You will miss out on developing a collaborative environment where new ideas and creativity flourish. Choosing to develop a Customer Experience Originator (CEO) work culture will provide the foundation your organization can use to build a rock-solid brand identity that will set it apart from others in the industry.

Your customers will perceive the experience your organization offers as a higher value, providing you with the opportunity to adjust prices accordingly. A word of caution, however: although your perceived value increases in the minds of customers, be cautious about raising your prices too high or consider not raising them at all. Either end of the spectrum can be risky. This is where it pays to perform good market research and to use the information to make decisions and create strategies for your organization. Recognizing that the customer associates the value of what you do with the experience you provide gives you a financial incentive to embrace the Customer Experience Originator (CEO) work culture. Customers who enjoy the service that your organization provides will share their experiences with others. This is one of the main reasons for developing an exceptional Customer Experience Originator (CEO) work culture.

A customer's perceived value of the experience will be the catalyst to encourage continuous growth and drive. A Customer Experience Originator work culture could not only increase your reputation in the industry as a leader and foster ideas that you have never considered, but also can add to your bottom line by increasing business and referrals. This can be achieved by the least expensive and highest-integrity advertising available: word-of-mouth referral by current customers who have benefited and enjoyed the experiences. When you have achieved this level, you become known for the experience—just like Disney.

CHAPTER 3

Most Organizations Fail to Invest in the Customer Experience

MOST ORGANIZATIONS FAIL TO take the necessary steps to invest in developing a Customer Experience Originator (CEO) work culture. One reason could be that they do not understand the value of the investment. They have not learned the difference that an experience versus mere transactional service can make. They may not be focused on getting things done, making a transaction, then turning that into an encounter that will be perceived as an experience by the customer. They never consider making the customer feel special. They consider everyone the same. They think of themselves as a one-size-fits-all organization instead of a fitted garment that is tailored for each customer. It is the uniqueness demonstrated in your organization that provides a competitive edge. Because many organizations do not understand this advantage, they are missing out on the chance to be more creative and innovative. This is an advantage for your organization. You can stand out from so many others in the industry.

Leveraging this information places your organization in a cherished position in which the customer's experience becomes tied to your organization's reputation. This is the type of brand reputation coidentity that Disney World shares with no other theme park. It has become Disney's uniqueness. It is what Disney World is known for. This type of connection of brand, reputation, and experience is the reason why at the end of the Super Bowl, when someone asks the game MVP what he is going to do next, he says, "I'm going to Disney World." These individuals are seen as super winners, and where in the world do super winners all go? Well, Disney World of course. There is no doubt in your mind, and that is the point. You would be surprised to hear the MVP say anything else. When your organization develops this synergy among brand, experience, and reputation, you do not have any competition. You stand alone and are known for doing so.

Some organizations fail to invest in developing a Customer Experience Originator (CEO) work culture because they think the cost would be prohibitive. This could not be further from the truth. In fact, some companies cannot afford not to make this investment. They think spending the time on Customer Experience Originator (CEO) will reduce productivity and become too time-consuming. My answer to this is: What is the cost of keeping a customer versus cultivating a new one? If you sit down and figure it out in dollars and cents, it costs you three to six times as much time, money, and other resources to acquire a new customer versus keeping a repeat customer.

First of all, your current customers know, like, and trust you and the end products that you provide. You do not have to tell them where you are, how to get to you, or how great the items you offer are. They already know these things. The real question is, are your current customers just happy with the transactional service you give or blown away by the customer experience you provide? You have to spend money, time, and resources to acquire new customers, because they need to know where you are, what you provide, and how great your organization is. When all is said and done, they still may not purchase from you because they do not know, like, or trust you. In fact, the Customer Experience Originator (CEO) work culture can turn your current customers into avid word-of-mouth advertisers for your organization, costing you nothing.

Another strategy to consider is the amount of money you set aside to attract new customers and determine your return on that investment. If you are not getting the return that you would like, then it's time for your organization to invest in developing a Customer Experience Originator (CEO) work culture. You will not only get a higher return on investment because of current customer referrals, but you will notice an increase in the number of repeat customers as well.

Another cost you should consider is the cost of losing your customers to the competition. Can you afford to lose customers to organizations that are providing something more attractive and are willing to engage them better than you are? If you answer no to either or both questions, then you must invest in the development of a Customer Experience Originator (CEO) work culture. To do less would make you the loser.

The Customer Experience Originator (CEO) work culture provides the opportunity to upsell your customers without them perceiving it. Your customers will feel as if they are gleaning expert advice from a trusted advisor, your staff member. This level of trust is achieved, because your staff has focused on establishing a relationship with each customer on an individual basis. It is the establishment of a trusting relationship that eliminates the feeling of upselling. Once this is accomplished, your organization begins to distance itself from the nearest competitor.

Many organizations never consider investing in developing staff to be Customer Experience Originators (CEOs), because they are unaware of the value of a Customer Experience Originator (CEO) work culture and/ or do not know how to get started. You have an advantage over them, because you understand the value of developing a CEO work culture. This book will help you understand how to begin to implement a CEO work culture in your organization.

One of the first places to start is to think about your customers. Who are they? Where do they come from? What is their educational background? Specifically what about your organization and the products and services you provide resonate with them? Why do they think they need you? Remember, this is not your prospective but the customer's perspective. If you do not know all the answers to these questions, then you must take the time to find out.

Have your staff enter a conversation with your customers. The conversation should be casual so the customer does not think your staff member is prying. It is important for your staff to show genuine interest and concern. You may have a staff member say, "Hey, Frank, you have been coming here for years, and we really appreciate your business. Why do you do business with us, and how can we make your experience with us even better? It is important to have your staff mention the word "experience" because you want to plant the seed in the customer's mind. You need to determine what your customers need and how to communicate with them.

I recommend that when your staff members approach your customers they start off speaking at a slower pace, make good eye contact, and smile. This will allow your staff to establish better connections with your customers up front. If your staff member starts off at a faster speaking pace than that of your customer, it may cause a disconnect, resulting in a loss of the message and sincerity that your staff member intended. Your customers may feel as if your staff members are rushing them or are preoccupied. Of course, if your staff member starts off at a slower pace and realizes the customer is faster paced in speaking, then your staff member should match the customer's pace. It is always easier to speed up your speaking pace than it is to slow it down. Making eye contact is key too. Some people will not trust you if you do not have good eye contact. Remember, the goal is for the customer to know, like, and trust your staff. Doing so will allow customers to hear the valuable information your staff will be sharing and see your staff as a team of trusted advisors.

If you want to ensure that everyone in your organization follows your lead in determining an intimate customer relationship, it may require a change in the culture of your organization. What are your organization's beliefs, values and pillars not only as they relate to the customer, but also from manager to employee, employee to employee, and manager to manager? Does everyone truly care about one another? If the answer is no, then how can anyone genuinely show care and compassion to the customer? If you are lucky, it may happen on a hit-and-miss basis, but there will not be any consistency or long-term development into a characteristic brand of your organization. Your customers will not have that Disney-like experience.

Your managers need to demonstrate to staff members the experience they expect your customers to receive. One of the best ways to learn something is to do it. Your managers need to show their staff how to create unforgettable experiences for customers by creating unforgettable experiences for the staff. This gives your staff the opportunity to understand the value of creating an unforgettable experience by sharing in the experience themselves. This process also gives the manager positive feedback and builds a stronger working relationship with the staff. It may sound simple, but are your managers doing it? I am willing to bet the answer is no, not consistently. If you answered yes, there is always room for improvement.

An area of strategic focus for your organization should be how your staff members treat one another. This is important, because the behavior among staff members trickles down to the customer's experience and permeates the entire culture of your organization. The customer will notice staff being cheerful and helping one another without being asked. There will be a feeling of collaboration and welcoming as soon as the customer walks through the door. Collaborative and welcoming behavior reflects high energy. So even if the customer is having a bad day prior to entering your organization, you and your staff have the power to turn the day around and make the customer feel better.

Having people feel better when they leave your organization than they did when they first encounter your organization is contagious. People enjoy returning to places that make them feel good. If this is the feeling that your staff imparts, you will notice more traffic and a higher conversion rate over time. People tend to spend more money in places they enjoy and become repeat customers because of that good feeling.

EVERYONE IS A CEO

CHAPTER 4

Your Staff Expertise Adds to the Experience

YOU CAN DEVELOP YOUR staff members to be the experts they truly are. People seek out experts for advice and help. When customers ask your staff members for advice, your staff members transition from being salespeople to problem solvers. It is the establishment of this level of trust, as we discussed in chapter 3, that makes this transformation possible. When your staff members provide this type of help and insight, they feel valued by the customers and find their jobs more rewarding. The majority of the time, people do not see themselves as experts, because they accept what they know as common knowledge, but it is not. Experts know something that the customers do not and need your staff's help. The information that your staff members share with customers will save your customers time, energy, resources, and money by eliminating costly mistakes. Customers benefit, because they do not have to try to figure out solutions on their own. Your customers do not feel alone, because they have your staff members as trusted advisors (experts) to help them navigate their journey into the unknown with a degree of certainty and confidence.

The time your staff members spend at work doing specific tasks gives them the opportunity to learn and helps make them experts. If your staff members worked in a department that had seven major tasks and learned all seven, they would become the resident experts. Of course, there may be some tasks that your staff members enjoy better than others, but if they are competent in all seven, they have become experts. It is this expertise that most people do not realize they have, but it is what your customers are looking for. Your staff members must understand not only that they have expertise to share but also the best way to share it.

Having your staff members understand their levels of expertise places them in positions to help more customers. Helping more customers will not only build confidence in the staff members, but it will also build a strong foundation for the experience that your customers will associate with your organization. Sharing expertise builds trust with customers, which leads to additional business. The best part is, the more that your staff members know about their jobs, the better they can help customers resolve their problems. When this culture of staff expertise is multiplied in several departments and leveraged by the caring relationships among departments in your organization, the culture starts to grow into a Customer Experience Organization.

Developing an organization where staff members see themselves as experts who collaborate with other departments provides increased value to customers' experiences. The CEO work culture raises the perceived value of the products and services your organization has to offer. Customers realize the benefits they acquire by having your staff's expertise save them time, money, or resources. Because of the level of trust and expertise your staff members exhibit, they are positioned to ask more insightful questions of the customer. Your customers will become more open to sharing information with your staff. Your staff members become expert partners, providing solutions to your customers' problems. The perceived value of what your staff members provide adds to the positive word-of-mouth reputation as a result of the customer promoting the experience at your organization.

Do not be surprised if some of your staff members undervalue their knowledge about their jobs. Have you ever had a job that you knew from top to bottom without someone showing you what was expected? I would guess not. None of us has had such a job, and your staff members are no different. We all require some type of on-the-job training. It was that training that provided us with the specific nuances about the job that helped make us experts. It is this knowledge your staff members obtain on the job that your customers are seeking. Your customers are looking for your staff to share the knowledge they gain on the job that will help resolve their problems. Your staff members may not be aware of this, but it is important that you invest the time and resources to ensure they understand. This information will help instill confidence and reinforce in the minds of your staff members that they are experts in the jobs that they do from the customer's perspective. Consider the wealth of varied experiences that your staff members bring to your organization when you hire them. All these experiences, years of schooling, and knowledge are what your staff members have to leverage when you begin the conversation about developing a Customer Experience Originator (CEO) work culture.

Consider the knowledge about the products and services that your organization offers versus your customers' knowledge about them. Customers come to your organization with expectations that your staff members will offer something that will benefit them. The years of schooling, on-the-job training, and work knowledge that your staff members share add value and help address customers' expectations. Would you like to improve the level of value that your customers receive from your organization? Ask your customers what they need. The more your organization knows about its customers, the better your organization can help them. Building trust between your customers and staff will lead to additional business, because your staff members are helping and not selling.

One of the best ways to describe this is from an experience at my local Lowe's store. I went to purchase indoor house paint. The sales representative was kind. He asked me about the current wall color. I told him it was white. He told me that I didn't need to purchase primer and showed me the various paints that I could use that would do just as well, which saved me money. He explained the differences among satin, semigloss, and glossy paint and showed me a display that offered color-matching suggestions. (This service is a real help, because I am blue-green color-blind, and my potential combinations might have been disasters.) Not only did the sales representative offer help, but he also saved me time (by not having to prime the wall), and resources (by not getting the wrong color combination), and money (by showing me the paints on sale that were just as good as the ones that were full price). This is an example of a staff member understanding the customer's needs and demonstrating his expertise.

When developing your staff members to be the experts they truly are, it is important that they understand customers' needs and the roles they play. The more you know about the customer, the better off you are. When I say "customer," I am not speaking in generalities but specifics. Let me give you an example. I flew into West Palm Beach, Florida, to meet my wife at the Ritz-Carlton. When I stepped out of the cab, the doorman said, "Mr. Thompson, we have a tee time scheduled for you to play golf at three p.m. There is a key for you at the front desk." He told me the staff had scheduled transportation to the driving range prior to my tee time. Needless to say, I was impressed. Why? I had never been to this Ritz-Carlton before. How did the staff members know who I was? How did they know I wanted to go out and play golf once I had arrived and freshened up? The answer is, they did their research. This event occurred more than ten years ago, and I am still talking about it. That is the value of knowing specific things about your customers. You will leave them with experiences that will last decades.

First impressions are lasting. My experience of getting out of the cab at the West Palm Beach Ritz-Carlton is testimony to the long-lasting first impression. I had never had an experience like that before. It is not surprising that I have told all my friends about it. Free word-of-mouth advertising, and, just look, I am sharing the experience with you now. After hearing about it, what is the first thing that comes to your mind? Wow! That is great! I would like to have that same type of experience. That is the value of creating an experience for your customer that leaves a lasting first impression.

Some of the ways you can discover more about your customers are through surveys and market research. You need to know the demographic statistics (age, gender, income, proximity to your organization, preferences for consuming your products and services, etc.) of your customers. You may consider offering discounts or specials for those who respond to surveys. Remember, surveys can be conducted online, on the premises, or by telephone. In your questions, you may consider what the customer wants versus what you have to offer to add value. In my trip to Lowe's for paint, the added value to me was the combination color sheets, because I am color-blind. Consider what could be the added value that your organization has to offer that your customers may not even be aware of. These added-value opportunities can also be a source of additional revenue and value to the costumer in an upsell. For example, the Lowe's sales representative asked what type of room I would be painting. One of the rooms was for my daughter. He asked me her age and offered suggestions for borders to go around her room just below the ceiling. I thought it was a great idea and returned with my daughter to review the selections Lowe's offered. This is an example of an upsell. I came to the store to purchase paint. I did not know anything about borders, but when they were offered, I considered and returned with my child to purchase them. Upsell.

One of the secrets of developing your staff members to be the experts they truly are is in their understanding of human behavior. Your staff members should be mindful of their pace when speaking. As mentioned earlier, if they are fast-paced talkers and speak to a slower-paced customer, the customer may not be able to comprehend what your staff member is saying. As we know, a confused mind does not purchase. I would recommend that all your staff, management, and you start conversations at a slower pace regardless of your natural tendencies. Then mirror the response you receive from the person with whom you are having the conversation. Slower-paced communicators need time to process and may ask a number of questions prior to making a decision to do business. A faster-paced communicator may be 80 percent sure about purchasing the service but may want to negotiate on the price. You and your staff have to be able to flex your communication styles to match those of the person you are speaking with.

The same flexibility is required when it comes to a person's priority. Some individuals are more task-focused and others are more people-focused. The individuals who are people-focused usually have big smiles when you first encounter them. They have to like you before they can trust you. Task-focused people have to trust you before they like you. They are observing your actions and want to see congruency between your words and actions. Both styles include knowing and liking a person prior to doing business with them, but they are in the opposite order. I know what your next question is: "Kevin, how can you tell what pace and priority a person is when you first meet him or her?" The simple answer is by observation. The most important thing you must do is connect with them without tripping one of the things that may turn them off.

Let's say your staff member calls someone on the phone. They do not have any visual cues to provide them with insight. Your staff member's focus should be on the customer's voice. If the customer speaks first, match the person's pace. If your staff member speaks first, the person should start with a slower pace and then listen for a response. If the customer is slower paced, then your staff member is positioned to make a connection with the customer. If the person is faster paced, then your staff member should speed up to match the customer. If the customer is slower paced and asks a lot of questions, this is a clue that the customer is engaged and perceives your staff member as an expert. It is now your staff member's role to live up to the customer's expectation. The staff member needs to be kind and cordial. Your staff member should not rush the customer. This slower-paced customer needs time to process the expertise your staff member is sharing. On the other hand, if the customer is slower paced and does not ask a lot of questions, the person may be shy or disengaged. Either way, your staff members should be kind and ask how best they can be of service. It helps slower-paced customers feel more at ease if they know that your staff members have a plan or process that can resolve their problems. If the plan or process is similar to something else that the customer might be familiar with, I recommend that your staff member reference it in the conversation.

This is where tone of voice is critical. You do not want to raise your tone of voice with slower-paced people. Raising your voice can be considered a form of aggression or anger, even when that is not what your staff member intends. Monotone wins out in this situation every time.

Having vocal variety with the fast-paced individual is preferred. If your staff member speaks to a faster-paced person with a monotone voice, the customer might think the staff member is disinterested. That may not be the case, but because you are on the phone and neither person can see the other, this could be the customer's perception. You want to smile when speaking to a faster-paced person on the phone. Even though the person cannot see you, your smile will come through in the conversation. Yes, you can hear a smile over the phone. Don't believe me? Try it with a friend and ask the person to tell if you are smiling during your conservation. You will be surprised that your friend can tell the difference. Some faster-paced customers may ask a number of questions of your staff. In these situations, the customers are confirming your staff's expertise. Other customers may tell stories about what happened to them and the reasons they are calling. They, too, are engaged, and your staff members should ensure that they have big smiles when responding to these customers.

There are specific physical cues that your staff members can leverage to their advantage when encountering a customer in person. If the customer walks in with a big smile and appears to be a snazzy dresser, the person is more than likely a fast-paced speaker and people-oriented. If the customer makes little eye contact and is a conservative dresser, the person is more than likely slower paced and people-oriented. Anyone who asks a lot of questions is more than likely task-oriented, and your staff can determine if they are faster or slower paced based on speed and tone of voice. Slower-paced individuals will tend to be more monotone, and faster-paced people will have more vocal variety.

EVERYONE IS A CEO

C H A P T E R 5

Embrace the Customer Experience

YOUR STAFF MEMBERS MUST embrace the concept of developing a customer experience work culture for the success of your organization. Your organization is at risk of losing market share to its closest competition. Even worse, your competition may find an advantage it can use to lure away your customers. Being second best is not a good strategy for any organization, especially not yours. This reminds me of the old Avis Rent a Car commercials. It went something like this: "We are Avis. We try harder."

What did this commercial do in the minds of the listeners? It framed Avis as a company that was suboptimal. After all, who wanted to do business with a company that thought of itself as just second best? Could it have been customers who could not afford the price and service of the first-place company? If so, what did that say about the customers who chose to do business with Avis? Were they the ones who were willing to settle for second best? This framed the brand of Avis to be less than whoever was number one. I believe this placed the Avis customer service staff in a difficult position. This meant that for the Avis staff to achieve a customer experience as high as that of the customer service staff of the number one company in the industry, the employees would really have to try harder (as the motto suggested). The perceived value of Avis in the eyes of its customers was already diminished by its positioning in advertising. Avis may have been better served and placed its customer service staff in a better position by saying something like, "At Avis, we aren't happy unless we exceed your expectations. We welcome you to be a part of the Avis experience." This would have framed the customer's mind in a different way. The customer is no longer focused on the competition's position in the market but rather on anticipating an experience that would exceed expectations. Would the general public have even known that Avis was second best in the industry using advertising focused on providing a customer experience? I doubt it.

Your organization is considered a follower, not a trendsetter, when the customers see it as second best. Once your customers form this idea in their minds about your organization being less than your competitor, they may still choose to do business with your organization, but they automatically discount in their minds the value of the products and services you provide—even if you provide the same services and products at the same cost of production as your competitor and charge the same price. Your customers will expect that the prices you charge for these products and services be lower than those of your competitor. This means that revenue for your organization may be lower in comparison. Making less revenue places your organization in a position to pay your staff less and invest less in business development and strategic initiatives. All things being equal, your competition may make more revenue because it has a wider profit margin (not having to discount its products and services). This will provide an opportunity for the competition to pay its staff higher wages (allowing it to retain the best staff and attract other high performers from other companies in the industry including yours). A higher profit margin provides the competition the opportunity to direct more money to invest in business strategy and development (new equipment, the most current technology, staff training, and rewards programs). Not having to discount its products and services to stay competitive in the market can allow your competition to focus its increased profit margin into targeted programs, as described above, to provide a more competitive advantage that can hurt your organization over the long term.

Being second best is not a good business strategy, because no one ever remembers who came in second; they remember only the winner. An example of this is the Olympic Games. No one remembers who came in second or third in an Olympic event. They remember only the winner. Even though the second- and third-place winners receive medals for performing well in an event, the national anthem of the country of the winner is the only song that is played during the medal ceremony. Everything is focused on the winner, and in a few years, no one can remember who else was in the race, let alone anyone who came in second or third. They remember only the winner's name.

The same is true with your organization and the marketplace. It is the market leaders that your customers remember. They are the winners, and everyone else is compared with them. These are the companies your customers remember. They are at the top of the mind when it comes to the products and services that organizations like yours offer in the marketplace. You want your customers to think of your organization as the market leader. You want your organization to be at the top of their minds in the marketplace.

If your staff does not successfully embrace the customer experience work culture, it can work to your organization's disadvantage. You do not want another organization to outmaneuver your organization's efforts to meet customers' needs. One of the best ways to protect your organization from falling into this negative position is to find opportunities to invest in a staff-development strategy. Many organizations will not hesitate to invest in machines or other equipment that will keep them competitive in the marketplace, but they hesitate when it comes to staff development and retention. One of the most valuable assets you have in your organization is its human capital. Failure to invest in the growth and personal development of staff can be a costly mistake that your organization may end up paying for in the long run. Losing a valuable staff member to a competitor can be costly. It takes anywhere from three to six months to train a new staff member to perform a job, and it may take up to a year for the new staff member to raise productivity to the level of the staff member you lost. The cost in lower productivity added to the costs of advertising the vacant position, interviewing, performing background checks, and processing a new staff member into the organization (orientation) can run one and a half to two and a half times the annual salary of the position. This cost can be avoided by investing in staff leadership training and developing a reward system for the staff you have in place.

There are always opportunities for the line staff and the leadership of your organization to learn new skills and ideas and leverage their collective knowledge in a collaborative environment. This is a great way to prevent the competition from getting an advantage and trying to push your organization out of the market or capturing your market share. Open communication from all levels of staff within and among departments allows individuals to identify issues that are hindering productivity and innovation. This is one of the best strategies for you to implement in your organization, but for it to be effective, staff members need to care about and trust one another. Learning about different communication styles and how best to communicate with individuals is an important strategy for everyone in your organization. This will help facilitate open communication. We have mentioned this earlier and will revisit how to leverage this knowledge in an upcoming chapter because understanding communication/behavior styles is key for your staff to develop rapport and build relationships.

At the very least, your organization is faced with one of three options: give up and give in to the competition, be willing to concede to being second best and following the competition's lead, or excelling in what it does by turning transactional customer service into experiences that your customers will share with others. Because the first two options are lose-lose situations, the best choice is the win-win situation of turning transactional customer service into an experience that customers like to share. When you make the choice for your organizational culture to move from a customer service mind-set to a customer experience mind-set, your organization and your customers both win. Understanding what your organization does best and working with your staff on how to improve it will help move your organization's work culture to embrace the CEO (Customer Experience Originator) process.

Take inventory of all the things your organization does better than your competition. One of the best ways to ensure you have identified everything that should be considered is to conduct brainstorming sessions with staff and organization leadership. An assessment should be taken of financials as well. What are your most profitable products and services? Is there a seasonal cycle that should be considered? Which products and services are the most popular? Are there any offerings that lead to additional sales? In what areas do you do better than your closest competitor? Once you have documented these items, you are in a position to identify your areas of strength in the market and you may find opportunities that you have yet to consider.

You need to know the answers to these questions because they have a direct impact on the revenue that your organization can produce. Remember, you want your organization to be an industry leader, not a follower. Knowing your organization's strong points is a great place to start. If you are working from a position of your organization's strength, you are working from a position of power. If you have not read the Marcus Buckingham and Dr. Donald Clifton book Now, Discover Your Strengths, I highly recommend it. It will not only help you think about how to develop your staff to embrace a Customer Experience Originator (CEO) mind-set, but it also will show you that a number of the principles they use and apply to individuals are transferable to organizational culture. Why? Organizations are made up of individuals. It is how these individuals think, interact, and work together that is the heart of an organization's work culture.

Ensuring that your staff embraces the Customer Experience Originator (CEO) mind-set is vital to your organization's success because you may lose customers if they do not. Customers have choices and are willing to exercise them more and more in the marketplace. This means you must constantly ask, "Why do customers choose to do business with my organization?" This question may seem simplistic, but this is an opportunity to discover your competitive edge or how you can pull away from the competition by transforming a mere transactional service into an experience. Does your organization make it easy or convenient for customers to do business? An example of the opposite of this is a TD Bank commercial. The customer enters the bank, which appears to be empty, and encounters a roped-off maze of at least ten lanes that traverse the width of the huge bank lobby. The customer starts to bypass the maze and walk up front. After all, no one else is in the bank, so why not walk up front? As the customer passes the entrance of the maze lanes, a voice that appears to come from the ceiling says he must approach the front by using the maze, in an orderly fashion. After going back and forth about ten times in these lanes, the customer finally reaches the front. He says he needs a deposit slip. The voice in the ceiling says the deposit slips are located at the entrance of the bank. This means the customer will have to walk the ten-lane maze back to the entrance and then return via the same route to do business. This is the antithesis of the experience you would like your customers to have. You want to ensure that you make it easy for your customers to do business with you. Is there any wonder why the bank in this commercial is empty?

Are your staff members who interact with the customers friendly?

Do they know the customers by name?

Do they show a genuine interest in what the customers want and need?

All these things have effects on transforming customer service from a transaction into an experience.

You may not have considered this, but your organization has made a financial investment in each and every customer you have. The money your organization spends to maintain relationships with customers and keep their interest can be significant and have a major effect on your bottom line. Allow me to illustrate this for you. Let's say an average customer spends $500 a month in products and services with your organization. This means the average customer spends $6,000 a year with your organization. If you spent 10 percent of that annual revenue ($50 a month for this example) to keep your customers engaged, it would cost $600 a year per customer. In an organization with one thousand customers, this would translate into a customer engagement cost of $600,000 a year. This is a significant amount to consider when thinking about investing in customer engagement and retention. The big question is how to leverage the Customer Experience Originator (CEO) mind-set to develop this investment into a transformational experience that your customers will not forget.

Transactional customer service is average, common; the customer experience is so much more. It is the experience that makes the entire encounter memorable not only for the customer but for members of your staff as well. Your staff members who embrace the Customer Experience Originator (CEO) mind-set feel proud of the work they do and feel good about the help and information that they provide to the customer. Your staff members will see the development of a customer experience work culture as an opportunity for them to learn collectively and grow together in their shared knowledge. A sense of empowerment develops, and your staff members will start to take ownership of the experiences that they help manifest through each customer encounter. It is this sense of pride fueled by the feeling of empowerment that gives your staff members the power to own and craft the experience your customers have in your organization. They develop a team mind-set when looking at a problem.

In the past, if an individual staff member had a problem with a customer, it was that staff member's problem. Adopting a Customer Experience Originator (CEO) work culture shifts the problem from that of an individual staff member to that of a unified team of staff members. It is this unified team, not the individual, that wins or loses. A unified team mind-set improves collaboration within and between departments, resulting in an organization that thrives, grows, and develops into something that is so much more than just a group of individual staff members. It develops into an organization with a supportive work culture that cares not only for the staff and managers but the customers as well. People who enter the organization can feel it. They become immersed in it. They become part of it. They experience it. That is exactly what you want to have accomplished in your organization. You want everyone who touches or comes into contact with your organization to be a part of the experience, to feel the experience, to have an experience that they want to share and tell others about. This makes coming to work enjoyable for everyone.

Problems are easily addressed when they are shared. This causes less stress, which results in better staff attendance. Sharing and brainstorming to resolve issues provides the opportunity for your staff members to develop a deeper knowledge about the organization and about what they do. Even more important is how your staff members do what they do and how their roles integrate in the operation of the organization. Your staff members become experts in their roles and in solving problems. They become exposed to different situations and moved out of their comfort zones. Work is no longer rote or mundane but exciting, interesting, and unpredictable. There is no telling what issues the team members will face each day, but the one thing they can be sure of is they will do their best to answer and resolve issues to the satisfaction of the customers. This is what being a Customer Experience Originator is all about: making a work culture that is fun, exciting, thought-provoking, interactive, empowering, and engaging and that promotes creativity and innovation.

C H A P T E R   6

Innovate and Stand Out from the Competition

A CUSTOMER EXPERIENCE ORIGINATOR (CEO) mind-set promotes innovation and separates your organization from the competition. Brainstorming with staff members in your organization provides the opportunity to come up with radical solutions. This is a great way to have all the people within your organization expand their vision and boost creativity. Sometimes we are limited only by what we have seen or experienced. The majority of the time, the opportunity to do better and more is out there waiting for us, but in our shortsightedness, there are things that we have not even considered. Sometimes the limit is only in our minds.

For years, Olympic runners could not break the four-minute mile. People said it could not be broken, and it became a self-fulfilling prophecy. Then one day, someone ran a sub-four-minute mile. Since that day, Olympic runners have been breaking the four-minute mile to the point that it has become commonplace. Why did this happen? I think someone believed they could do it while others listened to the crowd and believed they could not. It was an artificial barrier in their minds. It was their lack of belief that prevented people from breaking the four-minute mile. So I ask you, what is it that you believe or do not believe about your organization that is holding back you and your organization? Are you willing to find out? Do you think it will be worth it? I know it will be.

I would like you to ponder this question: What could you and your organization accomplish if there were no barriers? Money, staff, resources—nothing was an obstacle. Everything was possible. What would your organization be able to do? Who would it help? How would others see it? Where would your organization expand? How would your market approach change your business? What new or different products and services would you offer? Let your brainstorming go wild. Do not put limits on yourself or on your staff members.

What will your staff come up with? Consider asking staff members what they would do if they were the owner (CEO—chief executive officer) of the organization? What would your staff members do differently? What would they do similarly? In what direction would they take the organization? The most important question in this process is why. Why would they make these choices? What do they see that would encourage them to move in this direction? What is it that they do not see that needs to be considered?

When you get into these types of brainstorming question-and-answer sessions, I recommend that you engage a facilitator to assist in the gathering and coordination of communication and information. It is important to have free and open communication and free thought association in the room. Most important, if the staff members feel that the leadership does not truly care about their ideas, your organization will not benefit from the richness and value that will catapult your organization far ahead of your competition. This is not to say that this exercise would not normally be insightful, but the best results in transforming an organization's work culture are achieved when everyone in the room truly cares about one another's success and the collective success of the organization.

Another strategy to consider is shifting staff member roles. This is best accomplished among departments that interface with one another or depend on one another in delivery of goods and services to your customers. It may be worthwhile to cross-train a few staff members in each department to perform other members' roles. The advantages are that cross-trained staff members will be learning the trials of doing each other's jobs as well as discovering how others' roles affect their own departments. This insight can help them discover ways to streamline their work flow to improve efficiency in both departments. Open communication, a feeling of organizational teamwork, and pride without a need to protect territorial practices will be the by-products and returns on this collaborative staff role swap.

Another way to promote innovation is to research your competitors. What are they doing that you can do better? Take an inventory of the products and services the competitors offer. Where are they weak? Most customers want the products or services they consume to be quicker, cheaper, or higher-quality. How do the products that your organization offers compare with the competition's? Is this something that you can promote and take advantage of?

I remember that as a little boy, when I had only a penny or two, I would go to the candy store for one specific candy: a Tootsie Roll. Why? It lasted a long time. In fact, that was the tagline for the candy in the advertisement. It was true; no candy could outlast a Tootsie Roll. What type of Tootsie Roll does your company offer compared with the competition? This cross-department team role exchange can be helpful to identify the products and services your competition offers that your organization can deliver cheaper, faster, better. If you are not sure whether you have a Tootsie Roll in your organization, this is the best way to discover it.

Cross-department integration and exchange of staff combined with open communication and brainstorming can help your organization discover the next greatest thing that will push you ahead of the competition. You want to know what your customer needs and how you can provide it in the most efficient way. If your competition is doing a lousy job of providing it, that gives you an advantage. This is why researching your competition is important. But what if you find out that you both are doing an equally good job of providing the service the customer desires and there is not much room for either of you to make an improvement?

That is when your organization benefits from the strategic advantage of developing the customer experience. With all things being equal, the customer experience will win over customer service every single time. The CEO (Customer Experience Originator) work culture mindset that you, your staff, and your organization leadership develop will place your organization over the top and separate it from the competition. It makes the customer experience in your organization memorable and sharable.

Making the experience as unique as possible will contribute to your organization being viewed differently from your competition. Think of things your organization can do that will add value, not cost, to the experience that the customer receives. Let's take a small-business owner in a strip mall. He sells shoes. It is a rainy day, and the store is not experiencing a lot of traffic. Staff members in this shoe store have unproductive time. Are they serving customers? No. Then what should they do? Inventory and reconciliation of stock have been done. Orders have been placed. Everything is orderly and in place throughout the store. Now what? My recommendation is to have them serve customers. So you say to me, "Kevin, they do not have any customers in the shoe store to serve." And I say, "Get some." How should they do that?

This is where the brainstorming and open communication we spoke of earlier take place. If you were this shoe store owner and you asked your staff members what they noticed on a rainy day, everyone would come up with the obvious things first: low traffic and a lot of downtime. If you asked them how they felt about their workday and they were honest, they would say they were bored. If you asked them whether they would be bored if they were serving customers, they would say no. So the obvious answer is for them to find customers to serve, but the way to find customers is not so obvious. This is where the mind-sets of everyone within your organization shift to become focused on customer experience.

When customers come to this strip mall, they know why they are coming and the specific stores where they intend to go shopping. Consider what could happen if the staff members of this shoe store turned their customer service mind-set into a customer experience mind-set? If you take the suggestion I have offered about organization-wide brainstorming and consider no barriers to the suggestions that result, the possibilities are endless. Let me give you a few examples.

It is a rainy day. If the staff of this shoe store and the owner decide, "We are going to go out and get customers," then anyone who drives into the parking lot is fair game. The store staff and owner collaborate to develop a Customer Experience Originator (CEO) strategy. The owner has staff members positioned at the door of the shoe store to look for customers who drive into the parking lot of the strip mall. When they see someone park, a staff member is dispatched immediately to meet the customer with an umbrella and offer to escort the customer to any store. What kind of impression would that leave on the customer? The fact that these staff members meet customers in the rain at their cars to escort them to the stores of their choice and not the shoe store where they are employed would be considered amazing. People would start to talk about it.

Now, how do you make this a transformational experience that results in increased revenue for the shoe store? Have the staff wear shirts with the name of the shoe store. The owner may want to invest in umbrellas with the name of the shoe store. The staff members explain to the customers while escorting them through the rain that their shoe store takes pride in providing experiences that their customers never forget. That is why they meet customers in the parking lot. The fact is that these shoe store staff members are creating experiences for the customers without the customers coming to the shoe store. This Customer Experience Originator (CEO) strategy will result in piquing customers' curiosity to visit the shoe store in the rain. These customers come to the shoe store to continue the experience that started with staff members meeting them at their cars with umbrellas. This CEO strategy will result in additional customer traffic that the shoe store never would have had in the rain. It does not take much in terms of additional expenses. Remember, the staff members originally were not taking care of customers in the store; they had unproductive time. What changed were their mind-sets. This organization turned unproductive time and boredom into customer experiences and additional income. This is just an example of what can be done in any organization including yours. The possibilities are endless, and your organization is limited only by the imaginations and beliefs of you and your staff. So let me ask you: What can you imagine and what do you believe when it comes to your organization?

Want to know what your customers think or what they want? Ask them. Engage your customers in a conversation of what they would like to see or what your organization could do better. They will tell you. But it must be done with care and sincerity, and ask only if you are willing to hear what they are going to tell you. Surveys can be helpful, but you may get more information having face-to-face conversations. Remember, these conversations are informational and should not be confrontational. Having a script may help in some situations. You need to determine what will work best for you and your organization.

CHAPTER 7

You Don't Have to Break the Bank

YOU DO NOT HAVE TO break the bank to offer an amazing customer experience. You saw an example of that in the previous chapter. So let's examine the concepts and strategies used by the strip mall shoe store organization and how you can leverage the same type of thinking with the staff in your organization.

In the shoe store, there was an unmet need that everyone identified and experienced together: a lack of customers. In this instance, the brainstorming took a positive position, but it could have taken a negative position. For example, they did not have customers on rainy days, so they did not need as many staff members in the store. The shoe store owner could have said, "My solution to this problem is for one employee to not come into work when there is a forecast of rain. I'll rotate who that is so it would be done fairly." This might work, but the organization is doomed in the long term. The best staff workers will look for more secure jobs and leave the shoe store, which will have a negative impact on morale, productivity, and the service that staff members provide customers on sunny days. This is a belief of lack (allowing pessimisim to limit possible outcomes) and a mind-set focused on a situation that the owner and his staff feel is outside of their control: the rain.

Going out in the rain with an umbrella is forward thinking and in line with what the shoe store owner and his staff decide to do as an organization, creating a customer experience. It does not matter where the customer in the parking lot is going. This organization is focused on identifying something that the customer needs that no one else is doing, which adds value to the customer's visit to the strip mall and positions the organization as one that cares about customers—so much so that the staff members of this organization are willing to meet customers at their cars with umbrellas even if they are not coming to shop at their shoe store. This makes customers curious. The customers think to themselves, "Why would anyone do this? What kind of shoe store is this?" The curiosity about the experience that these staff members create is so strong that these customers feel compelled to visit the shoe store. The Customer Experience Originator (CEO) strategy that this organization uses manifests into acts of kindness demonstrated by its staff members, resulting in customers' feelings of being cared for and valued. The positive brainstorming provides the staff and shoe store owner the freedom to think beyond the lack of customer traffic and focus on providing customers with something they need. This new point of view provides the opportunity for this organization to discover a solution by focusing on filling the customer's need, resulting in additional traffic on a rainy day.

How do you ensure that brainstorming in your organization takes the positive point of view versus the negative point of view? One of the best ways is to engage an impartial facilitator. You need someone who has no specific agenda to promote other than partnering with you and your organization to achieve these positive results, someone like me of course. The advantage of engaging me as a facilitator is that I will not allow members of your organization to focus on things outside of their control or maintain mind-sets based on lack. My expertise is helping organizations identify opportunities to leverage and turn transactional service into experiences that customers share with others.

Doing this work and positive reflection, introspection, and projection will provide additional revenue to your bottom line and far outweigh the costs of time and money you invest in it. Making a decision to not invest in doing this work is almost like driving a car with your eyes closed to reach a destination. If the road ahead is straight, no one else is on it, the car is well-aligned, and you keep the steering wheel straight, you might reach the desired destination without an accident. But we all know that in life the road is hardly ever straight for any length of time. Pursuing this type of organizational work culture shift and mind-set will allow you to make up any perceived loss in productivity and revenue in the short run to far surpass what you would have been able to accomplish by the end of the year.

I worked with the staff of an organization that had the worst customer service and employee satisfaction and turned it around to be number one in both areas in a year's time. The Customer Experience Originator (CEO) process provided the foundation for staff members to transform the products and services they provided into something that customers talked about and shared with friends.

Let's discuss the return on investment. Before embracing the Customer Experience Originator (CEO) process, this organization had a high employee absentee rate, low morale, poor communication, and little to no teamwork. The staff members avoided problem resolution, blamed one another, received little or no support from management, and were known to provide poor customer service. The Customer Experience Originator (CEO) process improved communication among staff members within and between departments. Staff members developed a deeper understanding of the vital positions they played to the success of the people around them, the success of people in other departments, and the overall success of the organization. Managers demonstrated that they cared about their employees, listened to their ideas, implemented them, and saved the organization time and money while increasing productivity across the board. The staff members felt a mutual feeling of ownership and empowerment demonstrated in how they worked together, especially when faced with a problem. There was no more finger pointing, but a feeling of teamwork that resonated throughout departments and between staff and management. Customers were not seen as burdens but welcome opportunities for staff to share their knowledge, expertise, and the new experience that they crafted for their customers. Everything these staff members did changed from an individualized-employee focus to a customer experience focus. This shift in mind-set could be seen in everything these staff members said and did. They made each customer feel like the most important person in the world to them, and each customer truly was. Both the staff's and managers' mind-sets changed to one of taking ownership of the business and ensuring that their main goal was providing customers with exceptional experiences that they would share with others. As the customer experience grew, so did the morale of the staff. The absentee rate approached zero. Everyone looked forward to coming to work. The staff members focused on making work fun, not mundane, and exciting for each customer who entered. This not only increased revenue because of word-of-mouth referrals, but productivity also increased as a result of management partnering and listening to staff suggestions. The return that this organization received as a result of increased productivity, morale, and teamwork, combined with the drastic reduction in absenteeism and lateness, paid for the cost of training multiple times over with a long-term effect of transforming customer service into an experience.

The opportunities to provide an amazing customer experience are all around you waiting to be discovered. Have you ever considered asking your staff members to do one thing in a different way than they are used to doing it? The idea behind this is to encourage creativity and start them thinking about their jobs differently. If everyone in your organization thought of one thing to do differently to save money, help a customer, encourage better communication, market the organization better, or improve morale, you would be surprised what ideas will arise. The best part is knowing that it costs you nothing but the time you and your staff spend doing it. That time is not wasted if you consider it part of the strategic organization's development plan. Why not try it? You may end up feeling like Forrest Gump with his box of chocolates: You may not be sure what you are going to get. But one thing is sure: it will be sweet when you do get it.

CHAPTER 8

A CEO Work Culture Changes Staff Attitudes

EMBRACING THE CUSTOMER EXPERIENCE ORIGINATOR (CEO) process will change the attitude of your staff. Focusing on development of a customer experience takes the minds of staff members off of themselves. Your staff focuses on the most important person: the customer. It has been my experience that when people are self-absorbed, they tend to focus on problems (their own), but when they are focused on someone else's problems, they are focused on solutions. Providing a customer experience gives your staff members the opportunity to demonstrate their knowledge. Sharing their expertise provides value to the customer. Most staff members do not really value what they know about their jobs. Many may not consider this knowledge to be special. The truth is, it is valuable and special. That is why the customer is coming in the first place. The customer is looking for help—help from your staff. Your staff members' jobs are valuable because without them, the customer experience would cease to exist. Providing the customer with an experience, not just service, is a chance to highlight the value your staff brings to the customer. It also offers opportunities for staff members to expand their knowledge. The more that your staff members know, the better they can help the customer. It becomes a self-fulfilling prophecy. The more your staff members learn, the more they want to know. In time, each staff member will look forward to being the go-to person for the customer. When a customer is stuck or needs help, your staff member has the confidence to address the problem. There is a feeling of gratitude that your customers share with your staff member. This results in a feeling of accomplishment and satisfaction for your staff member. This fuels the desire for your staff to continue to create the experience. Learning more about what the customer needs presents additional opportunities for your staff to build on the experience.

This leads to your staff feeling empowered in resolving customer problems. There is a sense of ownership that comes with developing a customer experience. After all, your staff members have spent time determining what your customer experience should look like. If the experience does not go well, your staff has a vested interest to make it better. Ensuring an exceptional experience for your customers is your staff's goal. Management support of the Customer Experience Originator (CEO) process is reflected in the customer's outcome. A customer who has less than a satisfactory experience in the Customer Experience Originator (CEO) process will always have a better outcome than one in a transactional customer service work culture.

The amount of time your management staff members are willing to invest supporting the ideas and suggestions that their direct employees come up with will pay off in multiple ways. It is like planting a seed. Your staff's ideas need to be nurtured, watered, and cared for initially. After a while, they become self-sustaining. This is the difference between transactional service and transformational experience. Staff members, empowered by management, will look for opportunities to partner and brainstorm with one another to resolve problems. This type of staff collaboration has the potential to develop into cross-functional teams. These teams are willing to work together for the common good of developing an exceptional customer experience. The work culture of your organization will start to move from being reactive to being proactive.

How do you prevent ruining the experience before it happens?

Once your staff members' mind-sets shift to become proactive, they will anticipate or prevent potential problems. This places your organization in a position to outmaneuver your competition. Why? Because your competitors are not thinking this way. They do not have the open communication or supportive work culture needed to make these changes. Your competition does not have the mind-set of the CEO (Customer Experience Originator).

CHAPTER 9

So Excited About Work

EMBRACING THE CEO (Customer Experience Originator) process will contribute to staff members' excitement about their jobs. Turning transactional service into a transformational experience is fun and exciting. It allows your staff members to be creative and think about the products and services your organization offers in different ways. Your staff members will enjoy the opportunity to share their expertise with your customers and develop a sense of pride in the process. You may notice that your staff members are spending more time talking with the customers. This is not wasted time. It is an opportunity to deepen relationships that staff members have with your customers. One of the advantages of these conversations can be obtaining inside market research directly from customers by finding out what they need, want, or like. Your staff members get to know your customers by name. This is a value-added exercise that will enhance the customer's experience when your staff can refer to each customer by name. All of this adds to staff members feeling more empowered and appreciated for the knowledge and expertise they share with customers.

Spending time to discover customers' needs can lead to increased sales for your organization. When a staff member develops and deepens a relationship with your customer, the customer's perception of your staff member changes from a salesperson to a trusted advisor. When this transition occurs, the opportunity to increase sales does as well. When your staff members are seen as operating in the customer's best interest and not their own, the customer feels the sincerity your staff shares with them. Customers appreciate not being sold to, but prefer to partner with your staff to resolve a problem. Once this occurs, the customer will choose to do business with your organization over your competition. People want to do business with people they know, like, and trust. If your staff fosters and deepens this type of relationship, the loyalty your customers have for your organization grows and the comparison with your competition diminishes.

When your staff members realize that they are perceived as trusted advisors, their mind-sets shift to seeing problems as opportunities that they can collaboratively resolve. Your staff members start looking forward to work, seeing each day as a new adventure in which they have the opportunity to use their creative minds to enhance the experiences of your customers. Being creative provides divergence from routine, which normally makes work boring and staff members unengaged. Focusing on making the day fun and exciting for customers makes the process of work fun and exciting for the staff members as well and helps add to the engagement of your staff.

One way to enhance the customer's experience is for your staff members to share their best practices.

What works in which department and why?

How can the best practice within a department be leveraged in another area of the organization?

How can departments support one another in enhancing the customer experience?

Collective collaboration builds pride and teamwork and provides a foundation for the development of innovative ideas. Everyone involved becomes engaged in the process and has buy-in to make the outcome successful, because they have a sense of ownership. Another way to foster innovation and enhance organizational communication is to have a fifteen-minute meeting in the morning—a huddle. Just like a quarterback on a football team gets staff together to discuss the play before he goes out to execute it, I recommend that you have your staff do the same in your organization. I first learned about this strategy from a friend of mine, Bob Cooper, who wrote the book Huddle Up. I had the pleasure of working with Bob and seeing this simple, smart, and expeditious strategy implemented in various organizations. It is an opportunity to share pertinent information about the job they are getting ready to do. In addition to instituting it every morning, I recommend it when key issues arise and possibly at the change of shift or end of the day. It is a great way to communicate in a short period and promotes collaboration.

This leads us into thinking of ways that you and your staff can make each customer experience fun. This may be a topic that you discuss in the huddle meeting. How can you make each customer feel special? Remember to brainstorm and think of what you and your staff could do if there were no barriers to making this a uniquely special customer experience for each and every customer. You will find that there are areas where ideas intersect and what may have been considered outrageous becomes reality. You and your staff members might consider developing a strategic theme for the week to boost morale and add to the customer experience. This is limited only by your collective imaginations.

For example, you may consider doing something outrageous and fun like "different color sock day." There are several variations, but I will share one as an illustration. Say you have ten salespeople working the floor. Two salespeople are wearing different colors of socks, a red sock and a black sock for example. When customers enter, staff members welcome them by announcing it is "different color sock day." The staff members inform customers that if they find a salesperson who is wearing different colors of socks they get an additional 10 percent off their purchase. This sparks interest in the customer, who is off on a scavenger hunt. This Customer Experience Originator (CEO) strategy adds fun and excitement to the day for staff members and the customers alike. After the customer hunts around, a staff member may walk over and whisper which salesperson is wearing different colors of socks. It is like sharing inside information to the benefit of the customer. It is a win-win situation. The customers and your staff members enjoy it, but that is not all. The customers tell their friends about the experience. This costs you virtually nothing, especially if it is your intention to offer a 10 percent discount regardless. This is a way to offer an unadvertised sale in a fun and unique way that provides an experience that the customer remembers.

Using behavioral cues to connect with the customers is one of the best ways to improve the know, like, and trust factors between your staff and customers. The various nuances of behavioral communication could fill a book. A number of organizations have engaged me to provide in-depth analysis for management and staff members on the best ways to connect with individuals who have different behavioral styles. As previously discussed, when communicating with the customer in person or on the phone, you should start at a slower pace and mirror the customer's response. If the person you are speaking with is faster paced, then you should speed up to match the pace. It is always easier for you and your staff to move from a slower pace to a faster pace than the opposite. Speaking at a faster pace and moving to a slower-paced conversation seems unnatural. Because the intention is to build rapport, starting off speaking at a faster pace is not recommended.

Another great option in developing an exceptional customer experience is to consider what you and your staff would like to see if you were the customer. Placing yourself in the customer's shoes is an inexpensive way to give you valuable insight into how customer-friendly your organization really is. Secret shopping your organization can expose opportunities for improvement. Small problems that can be corrected quickly can tremendously improve the customer experience. I have provided secret-shopper services to a number of organizations, which has provided valuable information. One organization believed that the customer representative was a reason for its low customer service scores. My secret shopping revealed that the customer service representative was exceptional in the customer service she provided. The problem with the customer service scores was directly related to the service provided by her supervisor. Executive management knew there was a problem but identified the wrong person as the one promoting the poor scores. This is the value of secret shopping and developing a customer experience work culture.

CHAPTER 10

The CEO Work Culture Makes Everyone Smile

USING THE CEO (Customer Experience Originator) process to develop a customer experience work culture in your organization makes people smile. Ask yourself: Is the current work culture of your organization representative of the experience you want your customers to have? If you answer no, the problem may lie with how your staff members feel they are being treated.

Does your staff feel valued?

Are supervisors supporting and listening to your staff?

Do staff members' opinions really matter?

Do staff members have friends at work and care about them?

The way your staff members answer these questions has an effect on how they feel about being at work. If they do not feel valued or they feel like no one cares about what they think or do, it will be reflected in their work performance. You can tell a lot about an organization by just observing the people who work there.

Do the people make eye contact with you?

Do they smile?

Will they say good morning when they see you?

Will they respond after you say good morning?

You may think that everyone will have a positive answer, but it just is not true. I have consulted with organizations where the staff would have answered no to each of the questions above. Some organizations are led in a spirit of fear. People do not share what they really feel, because they are afraid of retaliation from management. In these types of organizations, there is no innovation, poor communication, and no room for creativity. People are unhappy about being at work and are looking for a way out. Even the best workers are not functioning at their full potential and productivity is down organization-wide. You can look into the eyes of some of the staff members and see hopelessness.

I share this with you only because I have seen it firsthand. This is not what you want in your organization. It can be corrected, but it will not change without the willingness of the executive and management staff members to have open communication and be honest about why they are working in this organization.

Are the executive and management staff members there for personal power and personal gain or for the betterment of the organization as a whole?

These are the types of questions that need to be answered honestly to make the CEO (Customer Experience Originator) process work. Some people's quest for power is so strong that they are not willing to give it up—not even a little bit of it for fear that someone will reap more than they do. These people are not and may never be customer-focused because the most important people are themselves. They are self-centered and self-absorbed.

An organization where the employees are not valued directly translates into a work culture where the customers are not valued. If the customers are not valued, they will choose to do business elsewhere, and your organization loses market share. If this downward spiral persists, your organization will cease to exist. The converse is true. Showing care and concern for your staff can affect the care and concern that the customers experience in doing business with your organization. Increasing the amount of care and concern that your staff demonstrates to the customer enhances the customer's experience.

One of the best ways to do this is to think of things that your staff can do to enhance the customer experience and show they care. I noticed an innovative approach in a local mall. The Chinese food restaurants in the food court had a staff member offer free samples to people who walked by. A number of people may not have considered purchasing a food item from the Chinese restaurant, but its staff member was strategically positioned to offer samples. Yes, it is a type of marketing, but it is more than that. It is an experience. The staff member approaches, makes eye contact, smiles, and in a sweet tone of voice offers the passer-by a sample. The restaurant staff is looking to engage potential customers and slow them down long enough to get them to try a sample on a toothpick. It is usually a bite-size piece of flavored chicken, just enough for the customer to taste and make a decision. I have seen some of these staff members with plates of two or three types of samples to offer passers-by. It is a low-cost way of advertising that has transformed into an experience. Let me tell you how.

The customer sees the restaurant staff member approach. The customer makes eye contact, and the staff member smiles and offers a sample. Some people do not want to be bothered, say "No, thank you," break eye contact, and keep going. The staff member says, "Have a nice day," and moves on to the next potential customer. The restaurant staff member understands the concept: not all people will purchase, but they all will take part in the customer experience. Even those who do not buy have an encounter and may stop the next time. Why? They may not be in a hurry the next time. They may be hungry and looking to buy. They are curious about what the staff member has to offer. What keeps these restaurant staff members in the game are their pleasant attitudes and willingness to serve the customer. The fact that these staff members are pleasant even when the customer does not buy means they have another opportunity sometime later down the road. Why? If this person frequents the mall and gets hungry, passing the food court provides another opportunity to be offered a sample.

Staff members' consistency of a positive attitude in the experience they offer adds to the likelihood that a potential customer will buy. Considering the human behavior model, some people prefer to purchase when they are familiar with something. Chinese food may not be their thing. But customers who have open minds, empty stomachs, and kind, courteous staff providing an opportunity may try something new.

Another option to add value to the customer experience is to send a card or gift coupon for the customer's birthday. This may seem minor, but that your organization remembers the customer's birthday is huge. It places you at the top of the mind and associates you with something that the customer enjoys. The fact that you offer a discount and think enough to send something shows you care and adds to the customer experience.

Another way to show you care, enhancing the customer experience, is anticipating the customer's needs. A perfect example to illustrate this was the offer of warm, scented towels at a restaurant in Atlantic City, New Jersey. This restaurant wanted to be perceived as an exclusive dining experience. It had wonderful ambiance, music, and lighting, but the thing I remember the most was its scented towels. They were warm and delivered with a smile by the staff. The scented towels set the mood for the meal to come. This was in the early 1980s, and no other restaurants were doing this. I enjoyed the customer experience of the scented towels more than thirty years ago, but I can still recall it like it was yesterday. This is the value and the advantage of developing a CEO (Customer Experience Originator) work culture. Wouldn't you like to have your customers reflect about the enjoyment they have experienced doing business with your organization some thirty years later? Better than that, have customers happily share the wonderful experience they enjoyed at your organization remembering it like it happened yesterday? Do you think that would be impressive? Sure it would! Do you think that providing the customers with scented towels cost this restaurant in Atlantic City a lot of money? No, it did not. So how did the restaurant come up with the idea? It was focused on the customer's experience and how to enhance it.

The staff knew that the customers would want to wash their hands prior to eating after handling money or chips in the casino (which can be dirty). This was an opportunity for the restaurant to anticipate the customer's need and address it. But even better than that, the staff figured out how to address the customer's need and make the process of doing it memorable. Having towels steaming warm provided a chance for customers to clean their hands at the table. Adding a scent to the warm, steaming towel provided a chance to enhance the experience with the customer's sense of smell. The fact that this towel was clean, white, and warm made the customer feel good, but the scent helped embed the experience in the customer's mind. No other restaurant was doing this. The idea separates this restaurant from the competition and has me still talking about it more than thirty years later. The goal is for you to do the same thing in your organization. Yes, you will have to invest some time to discover it, but when you discover your organization's scented towel, you, too, will separate your organization from the competition and develop an unforgettable customer experience.

We discussed in depth the value of the shoe store staff meeting customers in the parking lot with umbrellas on a rainy day. This provided an opportunity to stir up customers' curiosity and entice them to see what was happening in the work culture that showed so much care for the customer. And let's not forget the concierge experience at Disney World. I have had the pleasure of going to Walt Disney World in Orlando, Florida, for at least ten consecutive years, and the one thing that always impresses me is the focus on the customer experience and the attention to detail. My family and I returned from a long day in the park to a room with the bed made and turned down to make it easier to get into, but that was not the best part. The thing I will never forget is the piece of chocolate candy on the pillow. That was the wow factor that transformed the service into an experience. Having concierge service provided an opportunity to have a light breakfast, fruit we could take for snacking during the day, and cookies and tea in the afternoon. So regardless of when we returned to our room, the staff at Disney was focused on providing added value to the stay to make being at Disney an unforgettable experience.

Anticipating the customer's needs was also evident in a restaurant that I frequented in my old neighborhood on Main Street in Flushing, New York. It was called Bacigalup, and the owner's name was Stretch. What made this restaurant special was its attention to detail and focus on making each customer feel special. If no one was at the door when a customer entered, a staff member would rush over to see how many people were in the party. Then the staff would promptly seat the diners and offer a menu with explanations of the specials and how the food was prepared. The server would take the napkin and place it on the customer's lap. If someone pulled out a cigarette—this was the 1980s and smoking was allowed in the restaurant—the server would rush over with a light. The attention to detail was amazing. How did the staff members accomplish this? They worked as a team. No one had a specific job. It was everyone's responsibility to ensure that the customers had the best experience possible. The food was extraordinary, and the service which transformed into an unforgettable experience has me and others speaking about it more than thirty years later. Anyone who has ever eaten at the restaurant would tell you the same thing. I would bring family members visiting from out of town there to eat just so they could share in the experience. The staff members were consistent, kind, and courteous, and focused on anticipating the customer's need. The experience and attention to detail that gave each customer a special experience encouraged me to bring people to this restaurant. This is the type of experience you want for your staff to reproduce for your customers and make this part of your organization's work culture.

Did I mention that the staff members at Bacigalup's enjoyed their jobs? Everyone who worked there smiled, and the pride showed in their eyes. They all knew that they were contributing to a special experience for each customer and looked forward to doing it. They demonstrated their expertise. They were confident, caring, knowledgeable, and kind.

The focus was always on exceeding the customer's expectation. They recognized repeat customers and paid attention to what the customers liked. Customers raved about the individualized experiences and were dazzled that the staff members remembered their names and their preferences. The staff members at Bacigalup's developed relationships with their customers and made them feel welcome and important.

Is this something that can be replicated at your organization? Of course it can. This is what the CEO (Customer Experience Originator) work culture looks like in action. What do you think would be the end result when your staff embraces the CEO work culture and puts these principles into practice? You develop unforgettable experiences for your customers that have them excited about bringing friends and family to experience it too.

One of the main takeaways from the Bacigalup experience is that manners matter. How your executives treat the managers and supervisors and how they treat their direct reports are crucial to the development of an unforgettable customer experience. When your staff members take the time to show they care, it sets your organization apart from the competition. You could learn a lot from the staff at Bacigalup. The people were focused on the customer, and whoever was closest would check on the table. The glass was never less than half full with water before someone refilled it. Servers would keep an eye out to determine whether anyone might be ready for another glass of wine. They entered into conversations that were always focused on learning more about the customers, their likes, and their dislikes. I noticed that customers were comfortable sharing their stories with the staff. I would hear someone say, "Today is our anniversary" or "We just got engaged" or "Today is my girlfriend's birthday." Once a reason for celebration was identified, the server would notify the chef, who would make a special dessert free of charge. A number of times, the staff would know the customers so well that they would bring out the dessert they liked the most for free. This reinforced the idea of Bacigalup as a place that made people want to share their special moments.

I believed the Bacigalup staff members followed another CEO (Customer Experience Originator) work culture practice of looking at their organization from the eyes of the customer. If I were their boss, Stretch, I would have the staff meet before we opened our doors to the public to take an assessment of resources (what the restaurant had to offer and the specials that day) as well as attitudes (how staff members were feeling, what they had to celebrate, what challenges they were facing), because staff member attitudes would filter down into the customer experience. It is a good strategy to discover what issues are occurring in the lives of the staff members to help them provide the best possible customer experience. Your staff members cannot truly care for your customers unless you truly care for them. After taking this attitude assessment with the staff, we would discuss how to address potential problems during the day. If we became aware that a staff member was not feeling well, everyone would discuss the best way to support the staff member collectively as a team. It may mean each staff member taking an additional table to give the ill staff member a break. I, as the leader, would be willing to pitch in as well. Remember, our focus is on providing a consistent, exceptional experience for the customer. The value in having this assessment and everyone pitching in to help the ill staff member demonstrates teamwork and reinforces the pride that each of us has in the work we produce as an organization.

At some point, any of us could become sick and would appreciate our coworkers caring enough to help. This is unity and commitment, and those are the characteristics you want to have replicated throughout your organization.

Presenting a professional image is important in providing a CEO (Customer Experience Originator) work culture that is focused on the customer. First impressions go a long way in establishing the tone, so you should have a good idea of who your customers are and what they expect. You want your staff to be clean and well groomed. Your employees should be friendly, willingly smile when encountering customers, and generally be happy and excited about what they do at your organization. This will provide a good first impression that your staff can use as a foundation to build an exceptional customer experience.

Additional things to consider are eye contact and saying "please" and "thank you." Staff members often overlook these gestures. I have seen this all too often in day-to-day transactions. A staff member may avoid eye contact hoping that the customer will select a coworker instead. The staff member may not smile or look happy to assist a customer or answer a question, and won't even use the words "please" and "thank you." Ensuring an exceptional customer experience means good eye contact at the very minimum or your staff member will be perceived as untrustworthy. People are not going to do business with those they do not trust.

It is hard to be angry with someone who is smiling. A good smile is the best defense against upset customers and may be a crucial part of providing service recovery for the customer. Saying "please" and "thank you" will go a long way to making the customer feel welcome and cared for.

Practicing good manners positions your staff for the next step: developing friendships. As stated previously, not establishing a good working relationship with coworkers will inhibit your staff from developing friendships with customers as part of your organization's work culture. Care for your staff members, and they will care for your customers. A great first step is to get to know your customers by name. Being able to refer to the customer by name makes the customer feel special and contributes to a good first impression. That is what the staff at the Ritz-Carlton and Bacigalop's did. Taking the time to remember names made the customers feel like they mattered.

Pay attention to the details. It is the smallest of details that provides the largest value, because the competition is overlooking these things. Every time your staff members identify and act on details, they are widening the gap between the service your competition provides and the experience your organization provides. Placing the napkin on the customer's lap and lighting the customer's cigarettes as the staff at Bacigalop's did and having a tee time scheduled and notifying me when I arrived at the Ritz-Carlton are examples of paying attention to details. Think about what opportunities your staff can offer at your organization.

Sometimes the way you feel about what you are doing can be perceived by posture. This, too, is important in establishing a good first impression. Staff members who are not engaged may be slouched in a chair, have their legs crossed, or have their feet propped up. These postures do not say to the customer, "I am happy to serve you." The customers may feel as if they are interrupting the staff or the staff member is not interested enough to help them. This may not be the truth, but it appears that way to the customer.

You have to impress upon your staff members that they are like characters in a play. When they are in the public view or interacting with the public via phone, they are on stage. Customers are making nonverbal assessments and value judgments of ability long before they have a chance to say something. You want to ensure your staff maintains an engaging posture when in a position for a customer encounter. Even while you are on the phone, your posture plays a role in how welcoming and helpful you sound to the customer. With good posture, your employees will be able to breathe better and not sound labored or rushed in their conversations. All these strategies combined help develop a CEO (Customer Experience Originator) work culture where customers and staff members feel valued, cared for, and important. When your organization develops a CEO work culture, everyone—employees, managers, executives, and customers—smile.

CHAPTER 11

Your Organization Just Exists Without a CEO

NOW THAT YOU HAVE an understanding of the value of developing a CEO (Customer Experience Originator) work culture, I am sure you will agree that living and working in an organization absent of the CEO work culture is not really living. Your organization just exists. The CEO (Customer Experience Originator) work culture provides the opportunity for your staff members to understand and embrace the valuable roles they play in your organization. They learn the value of being experts in what they do and partnering with coworkers within and among departments to make everything work smoothly. Your staff and management become part of a cohesive team that meets regularly and strategizes together with a single focus: an unforgettable customer experience. When this change in work culture occurs, staff and management will find their jobs more satisfying and fulfilling. All members have to understand the value of their roles to the entire organization. An organization is similar to the human body. All the body parts play specific roles for a person to be effective. If an eye wanted to be an ear, having only one eye to see with would impair the body. The eye that chooses to be an ear would not do a good job of hearing because that is not its role. If the body had to depend on the eye that chose to be an ear for hearing, it would be doubly impaired, one less eye to see with and no hearing. The true value of the body is achieved when all the parts play their specialized roles and work together.

If the goal is an unforgettable customer experience, then each individual in the organization, just like the body parts, plays a vital role in contributing to that experience. There is a sense of ownership that comes with this process and pride in delivering a product or service with an exceptional customer outcome.

All employees understanding their roles is followed by all of them understanding that they are experts in their roles. Everyone has a function and a purpose that they are to fulfill to ensure an exceptional customer experience. The fact that your organization decided to embrace the CEO (Customer Experience Originator) work culture places you at an advantage over your competition because of the benefits of performance, productivity, and profitability that are waiting to be discovered.

The CEO (Customer Experience Originator) work culture is empowering. Everyone has a sense of ownership in the experience that the organization has decided to develop. Working together, developing friendships, and teamwork across and within departments makes people feel good about their jobs and happy about coming to work. Helping customers and being seen as experts reinforce this good feeling. When staff members are allowed to be creative and empowered and have a feeling of ownership, things change. Issues that may have been perceived as obstacles in the past are transformed into opportunities to work with friends to arrive at the best possible solution for the customer. This is where your organization's CEO (Customer Experience Originator) work culture separates itself from the competition. Work becomes fun. Challenges become chances to collaborate and discover something new. A problem becomes a reason for people to rally together and get excited about solving it. When the problem is solved, the sense of accomplishment of customer experience ripples throughout the organization.

After all, the customer came to your organization for the experience that you have to offer. Customers and their contacts will come to know your organization's work culture. This is an experience that only your organization can offer. Having your staff and managers place themselves in the customer's shoes and look at encounters with your organization from that viewpoint provides tremendous insight as to how things can be made easier for the customer. If everyone in your organization looked forward to each customer encounter as the best part of their day and treated the customers in that way, an exceptional customer experience would start to develop on its own. A briefing in the morning and debriefing at the end of the day of what worked well and where opportunities for improvement appeared would help keep everyone focused on achieving the goal of providing an exceptional customer experience.

Consider what makes your organization unique and use it to your advantage. There are probably a number of things that make your organization unique, but you may not have taken the time to sit and identify them.

Sometimes you are so close to your organization or have such strong feelings about it that you may need help identifying its unique attributes that can be utilized to its advantage. This is where having an executive coach or consultant can be of help. When working with clients, I look at everything from demographics to products, from staff to economic climate, to identify the unique attributes of an organization and how these qualities can be included in the customer-focused experience. In the process of identifying your organization's uniqueness, you may uncover attributes that connect with customers. These may be as simple as "We have been in business since 1957" or "We have been selected as one of the top fifty organizations to work for by U.S. News & World Report for five consecutive years. You may also consider what your organization's specialty is. What product or service do you provide that is best known to customers? Think of what you can do to enhance that product or service. How can you put a "wow" in the customer experience by centering it on this specialized product or service? Let's use the idea of a wedding catering hall as an example.

Many halls offer photography packages. How you could make this a unique experience for the customer is to have the photographer take pictures of the wedding shower at no additional charge. You may also consider making these pictures available for the bride-to-be in an online photo album that she could send friends and family to view via social media. The fact that this is an added benefit to the customer is part of the experience. In addition, it makes the customer feel good about the catering hall, it gives the photographer a chance to develop a relationship with the bride-to-be and her family, and it demonstrates the high quality of work and attention to detail that is associated with the catering hall. What we have done here is not only set up an experience but also positioned the catering hall as a place where the friends and family of the bride will consider for their own special events. In addition, any time the bride-to-be or one of her friends shares a link to the photo album, the viewer is directed back to the catering site in a form of referral and free advertising. There are opportunities in your organization, just like with this wedding caterer, that you can use to your advantage, and you are limited only by your creativity and imagination.

One of the best ways to maximize the customer experience is to think of what your organization has to offer that your competition does not, and capitalize on it. This demonstrates added value to the experience. One of the things that Costco does better than most other grocery stores is having people available to offer samples. As customers make their way through this warehouse shopping center with everything from underwear to TVs to household items in bulk, they usually visit the food section. A number of grocery stores are prettier, but Costco attracts customers with its bulk-size items, varied selection, and prices. Although the discount may not be large, it is the experience that keeps customers coming back. On a Saturday morning, you can eat enough at

Costco to skip lunch because of all the free food samples that are offered. Customers gather and discuss which samples they like or encourage other customers to try items. It is an opportunity for the staff to share information about the product and have a direct communication experience with the customer. I have purchased a number of things that I otherwise would not have considered as a result of sampling items in Costco and have told family and friends about them. This is the same type of result that you want from your customers. It is also a way your staff members are seen as experts because they share information and interact with customers. The customers benefit by learning about the product or service.

Understanding the value of developing a CEO work culture places you and your organization in a position of taking something ordinary and making it extraordinary. It also allows you to uniquely position your organization in the market based on the one-of-a kind experience provided to customers. You have learned about the value, the benefits, and the rewards to you, your staff, and the organization's current and future customers. Now the question is, what are you going to do?

SUMMARY

YOUR ORGANIZATION CAN BE seen as an industry trendsetter. Leveraging the uniqueness of your organization can separate it from the competition. Your staff can create unforgettable experiences for your customers. Your work culture can become known for fostering open communication resulting in collaborative innovation. Developing a culture where everyone cares for one another and takes ownership of customer outcomes will affect your bottom line. Everyone in your organization can be a Customer Experience Originator (CEO).

Thank you for the opportunity to share the value of developing a CEO work culture with you and your organization.

EVERYONE IS A CEO

ACKNOWLEDGMENTS

THANKS BE TO GOD FOR providing me with Grace, Resources, Opportunities, and Wisdom to complete this book. Writing this book helped me to **GROW** and positioned me to help others **GROW** as leaders and **GROW** their organizations and staff as well.

Thanks to my National Speakers Association New Jersey Chapter family, Rosie and Ray of Caring Communications, Pat of Bohse and Associates, Greg the Master Negotiator, Anna the Local Celebrity Maker, Sheryl of Sheryl Golf, and Alan of AlanBerg.com.

Special thanks to Mindy Klein, the Book Midwife, who kept me on task in the successful birth of this book. Thanks and gratitude to Joe and Dawn of Pici & Pici, who are a constant source of encouragement in everything I do.

Thanks to my family and friends who provided their editorial expertise: Barbara, GG, Melanie, Mom, Shari, and Shirley.

Last but not least, thank you for taking the time to read this book. Let me know how I can help you **GROW.**

Best regards,
Kevin

AUTHOR'S NOTE

THANK YOU FOR READING MY BOOK. I am passionate about helping individuals and organizations achieve their highest potential. Too often, people and organizations become complacent, stagnate, and fail to grow or change with the times. In this fast-paced world, that is a recipe for disaster.

I work with individuals and organizations to help them identify opportunities that allow them to leverage their uniqueness, tap into their creativity, and promote innovation. Reducing conflict, improving communication, and driving cultural change are strategies that I share with my clients. As a consultant, I partner with you and your executive team to help identify challenges and provide customized solutions to help you and your executive team reach your desired goals. As a speaker and trainer, I convert these goals into customized programs that achieve success. As a coach, I provided individualized training and consultation to help leaders realize their full potential.

Are you looking to improve yourself, your organization, or your association? Please contact me:

E-mail: Kevin@InspiredCommunicationsLLC.com
Visit: http://www.inspiredcommunicationsllc.com/
Call: 732-778-7847

ABOUT THE AUTHOR

KEVIN THOMPSON HOLDS A Six Sigma Black Belt in process improvement and a master's of public administration from Rutgers University, and he is an alumnus of Tufts University. A distinguished toastmaster, he was a chapter president and member of the National Speakers Association Chapter Leadership Committee, and Kevin has more than twenty-five years of leadership experience helping transform service cultures to provide unforgettable experiences. He is inspiring and challenges organizational leadership and staff to alter their mindsets and embrace new paradigms.

Kevin's expertise is helping organizations deliver sensational customer experiences through innovation and building rapport. He is an engaging consultant and professional speaker. Kevin's outside-the-box approach dazzles and delights his clients. He plants seeds of knowledge sprinkled with wit that make his programs memorable and enjoyable. Blessed by being a five-generation family member three times in his life, Kevin has a gift for connecting with audiences of all ages. Suspended from preschool for talking too much, Kevin went on to become the class valedictorian and has been talking ever since.

Made in the USA
Charleston, SC
03 March 2016